LEAVES OF HUNGRY GRASS

POETRY AND IRELAND'S GREAT HUNGER

VINCENT WOODS

This essay is part of the interdisciplinary series *Famine Folios*, covering many aspects of the Great Hunger in Ireland from 1845–52.

CONTENTS

Cover | Brian Maguire, *The World is Full of Murder*

Figure 1 | Miriam de Búrca, *Famine Sod from Tarmon, Co. Leitrim*

INTRODUCTION: HUNGER'S LITANY

Loss Silence Shame Anger Indignation Language Exile Renewal Blight
Blossom Politics Science Hunger Africa America Sea Canada Music Death
Bones Australia Starvation Famine Poverty Stones Soil Grass Nettles
Poem Song Hunger Holocaust Love Endurance Seeds Smell Potatoes Syria
Siberia Milk Meal Bog Lament Hunger Celebration Plenty Cunning Hope
Child Dog Road

Some of the themes and images that emerge and multiply in the poems descended from Ireland's Great Hunger link that human cataclysm to a world of suffering and injustice, and connect Ireland's history to the shores of the Mediterranean today. Those thematic strands and recurring images took almost a century to emerge in poetry: after a passionate and eloquent outpouring of poems during the Famine years, the Great Hunger was followed by a long silence in poetry, little or no word of hunger's catastrophe evident in poetry written and published in Ireland in the post-Famine decades, no single poem of significance in relation to the Great Hunger/ *An Gorta Mór* published in Ireland until the 1940s. After James Clarence Mangan, nineteenth-century Irish poetry veered towards the shadowlands of the Celtic Twilight, the people's recent history lost in the urgency of forging a nation's future. The decades since then have seen the slow shaping of a significant collection of poems that look to the Great Hunger, attempt to bear witness across time, question the reliability of word as witness, and act as a kind of disturbance on the well-fed mind of the present. That it took more than a century to shape poetry confident and courageous enough to address Ireland's deeply wounded Famine past is eloquent testament to the relentless power of the human need to forget in order to survive and build again. The words of Nobel Prize winner Wisława Szymborska come to mind – "After every war / someone has to tidy up" – but even as the grass covers over the "causes and effects" of war, the poet points to the vital role of the person who lies on the grass, a cornstalk in their teeth, "gawking at clouds" (178, 180): poet or artist going about the business of remembering the future.

This brief overview of poetry and the Great Hunger is the response of a poet who holds a passionate belief in the power of poetry as a force of insight and connection across time and space, as often neglected witness to personal or national life and history, and as a source of unexpected solace and renewal in the face of trauma, suffering, and death. The perspective I adopt is personal and particular, the lines of connection I make and trace are delicate, strong, and expansive. Poems transgress limits of time and place; poets make new worlds out of random moments, imagined memory, and conjured image. Fragments coalesce around an invisible core, and the boundless impact of Ireland's Great Hunger continues to echo in word and world far distant from the shores of a small island in the 1840s. All of the work I have read and quote in this essay remains relevant to today's diasporas and humanity's blank gaze in the face of hunger, displacement, greed, and death.

I have chosen not to focus on the substantial body of poetry written in Ireland in response to the Great Hunger in the years of deep famine from 1845 to 1852. Christopher Morash's fine book *The Hungry Voice* presents these poems in their fullness and diversity, gathering together over one hundred texts by writers including Lady Wilde ("Speranza"), Aubrey de Vere, James Clarence Mangan, Richard D'Alton Williams, Elizabeth W. Varian, and Thomas D'Arcy McGee. The many anonymous works include "A Vision of Connaught in the Nineteenth Century", with its free-translation epigraph from Orpheus "Et moi, j'ai ête aussi aux enfers" rendered as "And I, too, have been in the West of Ireland", and its nightmare vision of wild dogs feasting "where the corpses lie" (Morash 130). I choose instead to examine the poetry of restorative memory, the work of Irish and international poets who seek to reimagine the Famine past, pay witness to its victims and survivors, and forge links to a wider world of suffering humanity. Many reasons may be offered for the absence of Famine poems in the literary landscape of late nineteenth- and early twentieth-century Ireland: the almost mundane shock of the new social realities, the need to recover hope from the blight of wholesale death and diaspora, the eternal fact of new generations shaping their own poetic voice and concerns, the power of forgetting, and the seeds of guilt within the conscience of survivors. Whatever the multiple and complex reasons, the wheel of a century went around before Irish poets began to dig again the hard ground of Famine life.

The title *Leaves of Hungry Grass* is in acknowledgment of Walt Whitman and his Irish-born muse Peter Doyle, and a reminder of how significant the US has been in fostering poetic and artistic acts of witness to the Great Hunger. The inclusion of new work such as Eiléan Ní Chuilleanáin's poem "Maria Edgeworth in 1847" and Miriam de Burca's drawing of a *Famine Sod from Tarmon, Co. Leitrim* **[Figure 1]**, a visual poem, is a reminder of how the creative response to the Great Hunger is ongoing and vital.

THE CARTOGRAPHY OF POETRY

The slow rebuilding towards an understanding of the Famine past can be found in Eavan Boland's trio of stark and haunting poems, "That the Science of Cartography is Limited", "Quarantine", and "The Famine Road". More than any other living Irish poet, Boland has confronted the complex and painful past of the Famine and its human cost, making poems that hold a hard kernel of stony endurance, a power of witness through and across time **[Figure 2]**.

> *"Idle as trout in light Colonel Jones*
> *these Irish, give them no coins at all; their bones*
> *need toil, their characters no less." Trevelyan's*
> *seal blooded the deal table. The Relief*
> *Committee deliberated: "Might it be safe,*
> *Colonel, to give them roads, roads to force*
> *From nowhere, going nowhere of course?"*
>
> *"one out of every ten and then*
> *another third of those again*
> *women – in a case like yours."*
>
> *Sick, directionless they worked. Fork, stick*
> *were iron years away; after all could*
> *they not blood their knuckles on rock, suck*
> *April hailstones for water and for food?*
> *Why for that, cunning as housewives, each eyed –*
> *as if at a corner butcher – the other's buttock.*
> (from "The Famine Road", Boland 42)

Boland's poems map the flinty landscape of hardship shaped by the people who built famine-relief roads or walked roads of loss to their deaths **[Figure 3]**. The particular experience of women is central to her vision in "The Famine Road", while her unsentimental eye crafts a journey of spare and unclichéd enduring love in "Quarantine" (Boland 282), a poem sparked by a detail in *Mo Scéal Féin* by An tAthair Peadar Ó Laoghaire:

In the worst hour of the worst season
of the worst year of a whole people
a man set out from the workhouse with his wife.
He was walking – they were both walking – north.

She was sick with famine fever and could not keep up.
He lifted her and put her on his back.
He walked like that west and west and north.
Until at nightfall under freezing stars they arrived.

In the morning they were both found dead.
Of cold. Of hunger. Of the toxins of a whole history.
But her feet were held against his breastbone.
The last heat of his flesh was his last gift to her.

Let no love poem ever come to this threshold.
There is no place here for the inexact
praise of the easy graces and sensuality of the body.
There is only time for this merciless inventory:

Their death together in the winter of 1847.
Also what they suffered. How they lived.
And what there is between a man and a woman.
And in which darkness it can best be proved.

Figure 2 | *Women Breaking Stones on Achill Island*

Niall McMonagle's anthology *Windharp: Poems of Ireland Since 1916* includes, alongside Boland's "Quarantine", Richard Ryan's "Famine Village" from 1970, with its memorable image of the long-abandoned houses becoming mist, and Sara Berkeley's 2015 poem "Famine Cottages", where the poet in California carries a talisman from home:

Across the reservoir, deer paths lace the hillside.
In my pocket, two stones and a shell
from the beach below the famine cottages
at Rossahan.

Berkeley's evocation of a tangible connection to the old land carried to the New World echoes Boland's images in another of her poems, "The Emigrant Irish": "What they survived we could not even live" with "Cardboard. Iron. Their hardships parcelled in them / ... And all the old songs. And nothing left to lose" (158).

The haunted, unmarked, and frequently unremembered roads and paths of the Famine are at the heart of what may be the first poem of the twentieth century to directly reflect on the reality and legacy of the Great Hunger: Donagh MacDonagh's 1947 poem "The Hungry Grass" (7) is significant as a Famine poem, not least because it is well made and memorable:

The Hungry Grass

Crossing the shallow holdings high above sea
Where few birds nest, the luckless foot may pass
From the bright safety of experience
Into the terror of the hungry grass.

Here in a year when poison from the air
First withered in despair the growth of spring
Some skull-faced wretch whom nettle could not save
Crept on four bones to his last scattering.

Crept, and the shrivelled heart which drove his thought
Towards platters brought in hospitality
Burst as the wizened eyes measured the miles
Like dizzy walls forbidding him the city.

Little the earth reclaimed from that poor body;
But yet, remembering him, the place has grown
Bewitched, and the thin grass he nourishes
Racks with his famine, sucks marrow from the bone.

It is notable that MacDonagh's poem was first published a century on from the worst year of Ireland's Great Hunger, some three decades after the 1916 Rising and a quarter of a century after the establishment of an independent Irish state. As well as marking the centenary of the Famine, "The Hungry Grass" represents a kind of coming of age of Irish poetry in its ability and will to look back to the stark horror of the 1840s. In evoking the folk tradition of the *féar gorta*, or hungry grass – the belief that the hunger of the Famine dead haunted the living landscape – MacDonagh introduced a vital image of deprivation in the midst of plenty, and anticipated later literary imaginings of the Famine years.

Cecil Woodham-Smith's book *The Great Hunger* was published fifteen years after MacDonagh's poem, in 1963; and Seamus Heaney's powerful poem "At a Potato Digging" would not be published until 1966. When MacDonagh writes "The Hungry Grass", William Butler Yeats is dead less than a decade, his words still dominating the shaped narrative of Irish political and literary life. "Too long a sacrifice / Can make a stone of the heart", Yeats had written in "Easter 1916", where he evoked the name and spirit of MacDonagh's poet father, Thomas MacDonagh, executed by the British authorities for his role in the 1916 rebellion. Perhaps too deep a suffering had also made a stone of the memory, because one of the striking aspects of any study of poetry relating to the Great Famine is the strange silence that seemed to form around the subject in post-Famine Ireland.

Thomas Kinsella has commented on the poetic silence of nineteenth-century Ireland: "I believe that silence, on the whole, is the real condition of literature in the nineteenth century – certainly of poetry; there is nothing that approaches the ordinary achievement of an age" (Kinsella, *Prose* 32). The extraordinary poetic achievement of William Butler Yeats is notable for the lack of any direct reference to the Great Famine, although Christopher Morash argues that "when you work through Yeats' manuscripts, his debt to earlier Famine literature is very clear indeed".[1] It is worth noting that Yeats's first production for the Irish Literary Theatre, *The Countess Cathleen*, had originally been published in *Poems* (1895), his most successful volume of poems. This remarkable play, with its mix of realism, fantasy, and searching transcendence makes clear reference to Famine life, death, and religious politics. By referencing "The Countess Cathleen" in his 1938 poem "The Circus Animal's Desertion" – with its celebrated last lines "Now that my ladder's gone, / I must lie down where all the ladders start, / In the foul rag-and-bone shop of the heart" (Yeats, *Poems* 129) – Morash asserts that Yeats seems to be indicating that at least one of those ladders is planted in memory of the Famine.[2]

In another of Yeats's plays, *The Dreaming of the Bones* (*Collected Plays* 431–47), we find hints of the buried history of hunger and death from Famine legacy; here the references mist into mythology while considering the urgency of contemporary violent uprising. The bones of Famine victims may mingle with the dust of fated lovers Diarmuid and Dervorgilla and generations of unnamed dead, and justified

Figure 3 | Famine-relief road: the road to nowhere, Bluestack Mountains, Lough Eske, County Donegal

rebellion may flare out of dark oppression, but the poet's vision gives little room for consolation or easy political piety:

> *Dry bones that dream are bitter,*
> *They dream and darken our sun.*
>
> *Those crazy fingers play*
> *A wandering airy music;*
> *Our luck is withered away,*
> *And wheat in the wheat-ear withered,*
> *And the wind blows it away.*

The Dreaming of the Bones was written in the midst of the bitter War of Independence in Ireland and the so-called Great War in Europe. The bones of the Famine dead mingle with the bones of those executed after the 1916 Rising, poets Thomas MacDonagh, Patrick Pearse, and Joseph Plunkett among them. It is striking that their poetry, too, was silent on the Great Famine and the profound social change it unleashed. Writing within late Romantic poetic modes, the poets of 1916 consider the beauty of nature, the fleeting nature of time, the pains of love, and the thrum of rebellion and martyrdom. But it was the next generation that looked directly to the cataclysmic events of the Great Hunger of the 1840s, and named it for what it was.

There are many identifiable reasons for the silence of omission in the poetry of post-Famine Ireland. As Christopher Morash has pointed out, famine had left the poets of the 1840s abandoned by tradition: all of the great Irish-language poets of the eighteenth century were dead and the Gaelic Revival was still half a century away (18). The formal constraints of English-language Victorian poetry continued to shackle the poets of post-Famine Ireland and those writing in the early years of the Celtic Twilight. The Irish language, with its rich poetic traditions expressing grief, loss, and indignation, was already in decline before the Famine, and the vast majority of those living their lives in and through Gaelic could not read or write.

A fascinating glimpse of the Gaelic poetry of an earlier famine can be found in the work of Cormac Ó Grada and Diarmaid Ó Muirithe in "The famine of 1740–41: representations in Gaelic poetry". Their translations of five Gaelic poems from *Bliain an Áir*, or the Year of Slaughter, provide a vivid insight into a poetic tradition that had been all but silenced a century later. "Speranza", Lady Jane Wilde, published her translation of one of these poems in *The Nation* in 1847; it is a small but vital link between Ireland's famines and a wider world of literary history that her son, Oscar Wilde, would later visit Walt Whitman in America.

TRANSLATING BLACKENED MEMORY

A modern translator of Gaelic Famine poetry, the poet Michael Coady, has identified a larger silence, born out of shame and an imperative instinct for survival, as a force in explaining the absence of significant poetry on the Famine until a century after it happened:

The Great Famine is the quintessential modern shaper of our country I believe, from willing rejection of language to mass emigration and a deep social conservatism and a perversely rigid and controlling model of Catholicism. Also: a willed amnesia about the actual event. In times of social disaster and breakdown, and especially when people are starving to death, what will they not resort to doing to one another in their desperation? We hear about occasions of goodness and altruism, but little about the dark side. There is a significant silence; a suppression of conscious memory as in all atrocity or holocaust contexts. How did the survivors survive, and in some cases thrive? Ask yourself this interesting question: this great calamity is only a few generations behind us all. Had we not been given a selectively programmatic narrative about it in our schools and school books, would we in fact have heard anything at all of it through communal folk memory in our growing up? – though it may be deeply branded in the communal and racial subconscious. The deepest silence is always about the darkest things ... About the unbearable and perhaps the shameful. The other mysterious truth of course is that in order to live we must also learn to forget.[3]

Coady honors the work of translation achieved by Seán Ó Tuama and Thomas Kinsella in the 1981 volume *An Duanaire, 1600–1900: Poems of the Dispossessed*, to which he adds his compelling English-language version of the Gaelic Famine song-poem "Na Prátaí Dubha" ("The Black Potatoes" or "The Blackened Potatoes") (73–4). The text, sometimes sung in Ring, County Waterford, is that "rare thing", he says, "a contemporary and passionate voice (that of a woman) from within the Irish language". The poet goes on:

In Ring I have heard it said that in the past some of the clergy of the time disapproved of the poem/song on the grounds that it seemed to suggest that the suffering could not possibly be the will of God – as some clerics apparently had in their time viewed the calamity as a providential punishment for sin ... But I have no evidence for that clerical attitude.[4]

The song was attributed to Máire Ní Dhroma of Baile na nGall, and Coady's translation of the original (73–4) captures its stark compassion and deep grief and religious faith.

Na Prátaí Dubha

The black potatoes scattered our neighbours,
Sent them to the poorhouse and across the sea;
They are stretched in hundreds in the mountain graveyard.
May the heavenly host take up their plea.

O God of Glory, save and answer us.
Loose our bonds and right our case.
Give us life from out your heart again
And level the poorhouse in every place.

If it was sin brought this penance down on us.
Open our hearts and banish gall,
Anoint our wounds with your spirit's healing
And heavenly host take up our cause.

Too little we hold you in our memory
With the dark of life and its caoin of woe.
Oh Jesus Christ, lift this cloud from us,
May we see your face as we come and go.

The poor of Ireland truck with misery
With the pain of death and the weight of grief,
Little children scream each morning
From hunger pains, with no bite to eat.

It can't be God that brought this down on us.
The starving scattered under freezing skies,
Or the poorhouse door bolted cold and dark on them
With wives and husbands set apart to die.

Snatched from them without compassion
Were the children raised by them in pride,
Famished waifs tasting soup of misery
And no mother there to ease their cries.

Alas, there are those endowed with wealth enough,
Who do not serve the King of Life,
They abuse the poor who never had anything
But constant labour for all their time.

From early morning they toil unceasingly
Each sweated day until dark comes on,
Little gain their best can earn for them
But cold dismissal and tumbled homes.

Oh King of Pity and blessed Lamb of God,
Free us from this tormenting pall.
Don't let a single soul be lost to you,
You whose passion redeemed us all.

The King of Glory will surely answer them
And the Virgin Mary unbolt the door,
The twelve Apostles will make good friends of them
To share in plenty for evermore.

That day will show the true heart of charity
With the King of Heaven handing out relief.
The light of lights and the sight of Paradise
Will repay the poor for this earthly grief.

Figure 4 | Daniel Macdonald, *An Irish Peasant Family Discovering the Blight of their Store*

THE GREAT HUNGER AS METAPHOR

Patrick Kavanagh's ambitious poem "The Great Hunger" (63–89) was published in 1942, five years before Donagh MacDonagh's "The Hungry Grass", and it is significant in the context of modern Irish poetry and any examination of poetry in relation to the Famine **[Figure 5]**. Kavanagh was the first twentieth-century poet to use the term "The Great Hunger", subverting the term by using it as a metaphor for life in post-independence rural Ireland. Instead of looking back to the 1840s, Kavanagh scrutinized his own time and the small farming lives of his home place in County Monaghan. Patrick Maguire, the bachelor farmer at the center of the poem, is a kind of rural Irish Everyman, symbol and voice of a hunger for self-expression and sexual freedom in the face of family tyrannies, closed communities, and Church repression in the Ireland of the 1930s and '40s. Starvation is spiritual, sexual, and psychological in the Ireland of Kavanagh's vision, but the shadow of hunger at the edge of the frame stretches back to the blighted days of the previous century.

Though Kavanagh himself acknowledged that his work in "The Great Hunger" "is not completely born ... You must have technique, architecture",[5] his poem represents an important moment of connection between past suffering and living hopelessness. Patrick Maguire is not poor, but he is impoverished; his crop of potatoes will flourish, but his own seed will wither into impotent ash. In writing about the life of many bachelor farmers in rural Ireland, Kavanagh was, as Fintan O'Toole suggests, effectively mapping the long-term emotional and psychological consequences of the Famine "in an Ireland that had to learn to value continence and caution above all else".[6]

> *Is there nothing he can do?*
> *Is there no escape?*
> *No escape, no escape*
> *The cows and horses breed,*
> *And the potato-seed*
> *Gives a bud and a root and rots*
> *In the good mother's way with her sons ...*

Kavanagh's poem found new form in Tom MacIntyre's 1983 adaptation for the Abbey Theatre, its celebrated production of *The Great Hunger* touring to New York and Moscow. The Abbey production inspired, in turn, a brilliantly satirical poem by Paul Durcan, one that Kavanagh would have relished. "What Shall I Wear, Darling, to *The Great Hunger?*" (123) is unsparing in its updating of an unscrupulous landlord class who dress up to the nines for opening nights at Ireland's national theater, then evict any tenant who cannot afford to pay the rent:

> *You would think that it never occurs to them*
> *That it's their rents that pay for the outfits I have to wear*
> *Whenever* The Great Hunger *is playing at the Peacock.*
> *No, it never occurs to them that in Ireland today*
> *It is not easy to be a landlord and a patron of the arts.*

Figure 5 | Patrick Kavanagh picking potatoes, Inniskeen, Co. Monaghan

DIGGING – A POET'S OFFERING

One of the most iconic poems of twentieth-century Ireland is Seamus Heaney's "Digging", which substitutes pen for spade and transforms the ancestral labor of hard farm work into the creative force of writing. The poem does not directly address the legacy of the Famine, yet it is almost impossible to read "Digging" without a thought to the history behind and within its words. It has a sort of sibling, or twin, in another of his poems published in *Death of a Naturalist* in 1966, the more overt poem of Famine remembrance, "At a Potato Digging" (18):

Live skulls, blind-eyed, balanced on
wild higgledy skeletons
scoured the land in "forty-five",
wolfed the blighted root and died.

The new potato, sound as stone,
putrefied when it had lain
three days in the long clay pit.
Millions rotted along with it.

It is notable that Heaney read "At a Potato Digging" on the stage of the Abbey Theatre as part of a *Poets' Offering*, a poetry reading to raise money for famine relief in Biafra in August 1968. This event is significant in understanding the developing response of Irish poets to the memory of *An Gorta Mór* and its implications in the contemporary world.

Pearse Hutchinson and Thomas Kinsella were among the organizers of the *Poets' Offering*, whose goal was to raise funds in aid of the work of the Missionary Sisters of Our Lady of the Holy Rosary, Killeshandra, County Cavan "to alleviate suffering caused by the Nigeria–Biafra conflict" **[Figure 6]**. Seamus Heaney, Austin Clarke, and Máirtín Ó Direáin shared the stage with Kinsella and Hutchinson; and a program note by another of the organizers, John Horgan, tells us that the poets' presence "is the articulation of a commitment which will, they hope, find a fuller expression in the

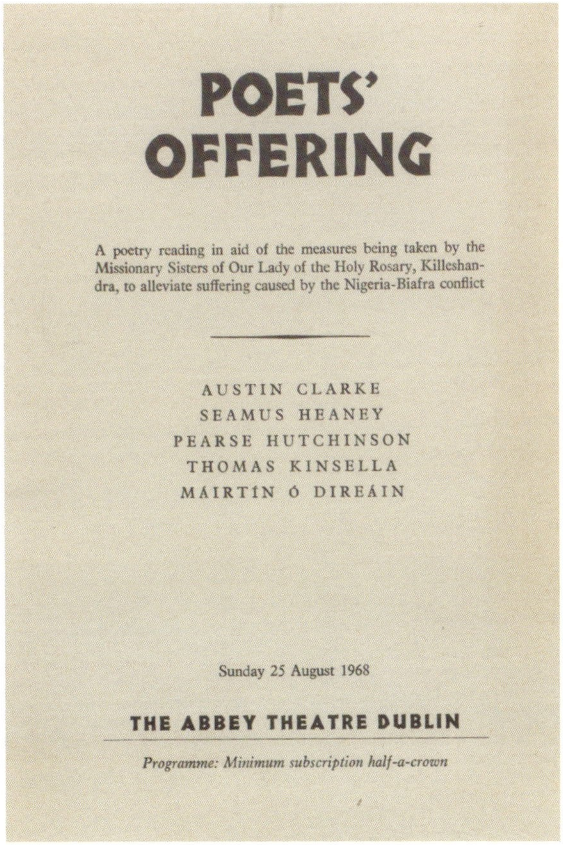

POETS' OFFERING

A poetry reading in aid of the measures being taken by the Missionary Sisters of Our Lady of the Holy Rosary, Killeshandra, to alleviate suffering caused by the Nigeria-Biafra conflict

AUSTIN CLARKE
SEAMUS HEANEY
PEARSE HUTCHINSON
THOMAS KINSELLA
MÁIRTÍN Ó DIREÁIN

Sunday 25 August 1968

THE ABBEY THEATRE DUBLIN

Programme: Minimum subscription half-a-crown

Figure 6 | Program for *Poet's Offering*

collective conscience of mankind". In words that seem acutely relevant to Ireland's past, Horgan writes that "hunger remorselessly creates its own politics – politics in which we are all involved, if we are not to allow people to starve to death without doing anything to help them". Emphasizing the strictly non-political nature of the event, Horgan makes clear that the poets' gathering and reading was "deeply concerned with the more basic politics of life, death, and shared responsibility for human welfare".[7]

The presence of Thomas Kinsella as organizer and reader at this event is testament to his quiet, passionate, and consistent act of witness to Ireland's hungry past and the loss and language seeded within it. Kinsella's work seldom addresses the Famine directly, but his poems are saturated with a sense of desolation and accumulated grief that seems to hold a deep layer of the wounded past. Just as Eavan Boland has written poems of direct confrontation with the Famine and its shadows, Kinsella makes poems that hold history within them in a kind of mute witness that parallels the very silence he has identified and named. As Adrienne Leavy has written,

another key aspect of Kinsella's Jungian-influenced poetry is the manner in which he often frames his personal journey into the Jungian Land of the Dead within the context of Irish history and mythology. This creative incorporation ... is part of the poet's ongoing project of repossessing an aesthetic Gaelic culture which Kinsella views as lost after the death of the Irish language with the Famine in the 19th century.[8]

A new beginning. An entire new world
floating on the ocean like a cloud,
distilled from sunlight and the crests of foam.

We are all thieves. In search of a land without sin,
that might go unpunished. And so prowling
the Northern portion of the known world,
toward the West (thinking
places answering each other on Earth
might answer in nature).

Late afternoon we came in sight
of promontories beautiful beyond description
and saw the sea gather in savage currents
and dash itself against the cliffs.

By twilight everything was destroyed
the only survivors a shoal of women
spilled onto the shingle, and one man
that soon – as they lifted themselves up
and looked about them in the dusk –
they silently surrounded.

Paradise. No serpents. No noxious beasts
No lions. No toads. No injurious rats
or dragons or scorpions. Only the she-wolf.

Perpetual twilight. A last outpost in the gloom.
A land of the dead.
Sometimes an otherworldly music sounded on the wind.

Above the landing place the grass shivered
in the thin shale at the top of the path
never again disturbed. Where the sun went down
there was a great rock in the sea.
The Hag. Squatting on the water,
her muzzle staring up at nothing.

*

I must remember
and be able some time to explain.

There is nothing here for sustenance.

> *Hair. Claws. Grey.*
> *Naked. Wretch. Wither.*
> (from "Survivor" in " From the Land of the Dead", Kinsella 111–12)

Pearse Hutchinson, Kinsella's fellow-poet organizer of the Abbey Theatre reading, was no less keenly aware of the history of Ireland's Great Hunger, and drew parallels between Irish and Scottish experience of hunger and forced migration in his 1975 poem "Pibroch" (74):

> *Boarding the coffin-ship for Canada,*
> *paying their pittance to the foreign owners,*
> *the clansmen found their piper lacked even that.*
> *[...]*
> *So the people in their need scraped around in their poverty*
> *and mustered the pittance for the music to travel,*
> *[...]*
> *lamentation swabbed the landless deck,*
> *the creaking, rotting boat was outraged and blest.*

Hutchinson's poem "An Gorta"(Hutchinson, *Archive*) renders a fragment of folk memory into verse:

An Gorta (do Chatal Póirtéir)	The Famine (for Cathal Póirtéir)
An bhean ina luí marbh, *an leanbh beag ag siúl uirthi* *is é ag caoineadh leis an ocras*	*The woman lying dead* *the small boy walking on her corpse* *crying with the hunger*
Chualas go raibh páiste ag ól *Bainne cí a mháthar* *is iad araon marbh*	*I heard a child was drinking* *Milk from its mother's breast* *the two of them already dead*

Hutchinson's poem of bare witness (based on material in the archives of the then Department of Irish Folklore, University College, Dublin, which informed a series of radio programs made by Cathal Póirtéir) is impersonal, detached, a kind of poetic reportage. By contrast, Belfast poet John Hewitt adopts a distinctly personal tone in reporting a story of famine handed down in his family. His poem "The Scar" (177) is a masterpiece of linked time, human empathy, family history, and personal identity.

The Scar

There's not a chance now that I might recover
one syllable of what that sick man said,
tapping upon my great-grandmother's shutter,
and begging, I was told, a piece of bread;
for on his tainted breath there hung infection
rank from the cabins of the stricken west,
the spores from black potato-stalks, the spittle
mottled with poison in his rattling chest;
but she who, by her nature, quickly answered,
accepted in return the famine-fever;
and that chance meeting, that brief confrontation,
conscribed me of the Irishry for ever.

Though much I cherish lies outside their vision,
and much they prize I have no claim to share,
yet in that woman's death I found my nation;
the old wound aches and shews its fellow scar.

Hewitt's use of the term "Irishry" in "The Scar" is an interesting echo of Yeats in "Under Ben Bulben" ("That we in coming days may be / Still the indomitable Irishry"). In the double vision of Hewitt and Yeats, the term "Irishry" could be seen to extend through time and beyond nationality, encompassing the spirit, voices, and lives of the Irish diaspora, and asserting the right of multiple and complex Irish identities to live together on a small island.

Hewitt is unique among Irish poets in forging a declaration of personal identity out of a memory of fatal hunger, disease, and ancestral generosity; yet his deeply personal sense of a shared "nation" of scarred survival articulates something seeded deep within the wider field of Famine poetry. Famine history squats in the landscape, resonates in unexpected tones, and rings deep into individual and collective consciousness, as in this poem by Kilkenny-born Tom French (76):

A Cauldron in Dunshaughlin
i.m. Michael Kenny (1926–2013)

At rest with its mouth,
because it looked
so like an upturned bell
bolted to the ground

in Dunshaughlin
I struck that famine cauldron
with my bare hand
and it is ringing still.

A LOOSENED SPIRIT: POETRY AND DIASPORA

The poetic voice of the post-Famine diaspora is a rich and still-unfolding story. The hundreds of thousands of people who left Ireland for America, Canada, and Australia in those bleak years brought a gift of language, music, and myth to a wider world, and it is remarkable that two of the great figures of nineteenth-century American poetry, Walt Whitman and Emily Dickinson, were inspired and influenced by those who were born in Ireland during the early years of the Famine and who left for America in the early 1850s. Peter Doyle from Limerick and Margaret Maher from Tipperary became muses of a kind, he to Whitman and she to Dickinson. There is no doubt that the presence of two post-Famine Irish immigrants influenced decisively the lives and writing of these most American of poets.

Whitman's knowledge of Irish life, politics, and the unfolding Famine is evident in an editorial he wrote for the *Brooklyn Daily Eagle* in June 1846, when he takes the Native American Party to task for its anti-foreigner position on emigration.

There is too much mankind, and too little earth. – What horrors are every month to be seen in Ireland from Bantry Bay to the Giant's Causeway! What wretchedness in the hovels of the poor peasants! What grief and hunger have reigned among her people ever since Castlereagh and Pitt consummated the atrocity of "the Union"! (qtd. in Krieg 41)

The great poet of democracy would write directly on the Irish Famine and its American legacy in a poem published in the *New York Leader* on November 2, 1861:

Old Ireland

FAR hence, amid an isle of wondrous beauty,
Crouching over a grave, an ancient, sorrowful mother,
Once a queen – now lean and tatter'd, seated on the ground,
Her old white hair drooping dishevel'd round her shoulders;
At her feet fallen an unused royal harp,
Long silent – she too long silent – mourning her shrouded hope and heir;
Of all the earth her heart most full of sorrow, because most full of love.

Yet a word, ancient mother;
You need crouch there no longer on the cold ground, with forehead between your knees;
O you need not sit there, veil'd in your old white hair, so dishevel'd;
For know you, the one you mourn is not in that grave;
It was an illusion – the heir, the son you love, was not really dead;
The Lord is not dead – he is risen again, young and strong, in another country;
Even while you wept there by your fallen harp, by the grave,
What you wept for, was translated, pass'd from the grave,
The winds favor'd, and the sea sail'd it,
And now with rosy and new blood,
Moves to-day an armed man in a new country.

When Whitman published "Old Ireland" in *Drum-taps* four years later, in October 1865, the last line was changed to omit any reference to arms or potential uprising, and grieving Ireland's son and heir now simply "Moves to-day in a new country" (Whitman 334). There is no clear indication of why Whitman cut the original reference to "an armed man". It is possible that he was originally appealing to members of the Fenian Brotherhood (set up in 1858), who were being actively solicited for service in the Union army. But it was also in 1865 that he met his heart's companion, Peter Doyle, who was born in Limerick in 1843 and whose family emigrated to the US in 1852. Doyle became one of the central figures in Whitman's life, and the poet's close friendship with him and other Irishmen – William Douglas O'Connor and John Boyle O'Reilly among them – consolidated the poet's passionate interest in Ireland and Irish immigrant life in America. Peter Doyle was present in Ford's Theater in Washington DC on the night Abraham Lincoln was assassinated (Good Friday, April 15, 1865), and it is possible that Whitman may have cut the reference to "an armed man" in light of Lincoln's murder. It is believed that Doyle's account of his family's dangerous sea voyage to America (the ship, the *William Patten*, almost sank on Good Friday, April 9, 1852) helped to inspire Whitman's elegy for Lincoln, "O Captain! My Captain!" (Murray, *Pete the Great* 15).

Emily Dickinson's Irish muse was born near Kilcash in south Tipperary in 1841, and traveled with her family to America in 1854. It is thanks to the work of Aífe Murray in her book *Maid as Muse: How Servants Changed Emily Dickinson's Life and Language* that we know the details of Margaret Maher's life, and see how her presence in the Dickinson household inspired Emily's writing. Murray makes a very convincing case that Maher's Irish-English (some of it documented in notes and letters) influenced Dickinson's daring, experimental syntax; and while there is no evidence of Maher having carried stories of the Irish Famine to New England, it is hard to believe that some tint of news from Ireland is not present in Dickinson's haunting poems of death and endurance. Dickinson chose six Irish laborers to carry her coffin – an image that becomes a poem in itself: "When taboos are broken – as when a wealthy white Protestant Yankee chooses six poor Irish Catholic labourers for her pallbearers – there is something to be gained by looking at these cleavings" (Murray, *Maid as Muse* 24).

Murray has looked in detail at these cleavings, and finds a poem by Dickinson written on the back of a note from Margaret Maher believed to have been written in autumn 1882 when the Irish woman was recovering from typhoid fever (110–11):

Figure 7 | Lilian Lucy Davidson, *Gorta*

He ate and
drank the
precious Words –
His Spirit grew
robust –
He knew no more
that he was poor,
nor that his
frame was
Dust –
He danced
along the dingy
Days
And this Bequest
of Wings
Was but a Book –
What Liberty
A loosened Spirit
brings –

It seems Margaret Maher saved Dickinson's poems for the future, despite having promised to burn them after the poet's death.[9] The deep friendship between the two women inspired the novel *Miss Emily* by Irish poet and novelist Nuala O'Connor, who usually writes under the name Nuala Ní Chonchúir. Her account of Dickinson's friendship with Irish immigrant Ada Concannon has the dedication "For Emily, for poetry".

Dickinson's New England contemporary, Henry David Thoreau, was a witness to the consequences of Ireland's Great Hunger, and, in a scene reminiscent of modern-day migrant tragedies in the Mediterranean, walked the beach at Cohasset, Massachusetts in October 1849 viewing the bodies of Irish emigrants who drowned when the *St. John* foundered close to the coast. The poet noted the bodies of the known dead in boxes marked with chalk, and that of an unknown young woman who "probably had intended to go out to service in some American family" lying beneath "some hastily thrown cloths" (qtd. in Krieg 95).

In her study *Walt Whitman and the Irish*, Joann P. Krieg details how Thoreau was moved by the poverty of a small Irish boy, John Riordan, whose mother had patched his ragged clothes with countless pieces taken from an old pair of trousers discarded by the poet. In February 1852 he brought a new cloak to the child, and notes in his journal that the Irish are not succeeding so ill after all: "The little boy goes to primary school and proves a forward boy there" (qtd. in Krieg 95). However, as Krieg notes, a small poem in Thoreau's journal paints a bleak picture of the poet's expectations for boys like Riordan (qtd. in Krieg 96):

I am the little Irish boy
That lives in the shanty
I am four years old today
And shall soon be one and twenty
I shall grow up
And be a great man
And shovel all day
As hard as I can

AUSTRALIA: DIAMONDS ON A DUCHESS

The Great Famine in Ireland provoked poems of indignation, protest, and lament in other countries. One of the most notable poems published at the time outside of Ireland is the brilliant polemic "The Famine in Ireland", published under the pseudonym "B. R" in the *Port Phillip Herald*, Melbourne, Australia on June 17, 1847 (qtd. in Burke & Woods 29):

> *[....]*
> *To London, that opulent Queen of the waters,*
> *Thy titled nobility crowd from thy shore,*
> *While famine, more fearful than ages of slaughter*
> *Is heralding death to each cottager's door.*
>
> *At royalty's levees the robbers assemble,*
> *To kneel at the feet of an image of clay,*
> *While their tenantry's cries make humanity tremble;*
> *The smile of a queen heaps churchyards with their prey.*
> *[....]*
> *A countess pays more for the latest French model*
> *Than twenty poor families crave in their need,*
> *The diamonds that gleam on a duchess's noddle*
> *Expended on bread half the nations might feed.*
>
> *The thousands we squander to pamper the German,*
> *The millions that over-fed churchmen consume,*
> *The stipends of pensioners, spies and state vermin,*
> *Would save thee, unfortunate isle, from thy doom.*

The class-conscious political anger of this poem is unusual in its directness and its astute targeting of monarchy, Church, and state officials and administrators. I have not been able to establish the identity of "B. R.", who also published another Famine poem, "The Irish Mother to Her Child" in the *Port Phillip Patriot and Morning*

Advertiser in August 1847, and who may have written an acrostic poem for Daniel O'Connell and "The Famine in Ireland" (a different text to that quoted above) published in the *Port Phillip Herald* under the pen names "Anon." and "An Irishman" in October and May 1847.

Where bread is so scarce that the peasant to gain it
Will risk his destruction by powder and ball,
Preferring much rather to die by the bayonet
Than by the keen-cravings of hunger to fall.
[....]
Oh! Erin my country, I feel for thy sorrow,
And while a lone shilling remains in my purse,
Thou shall never beg from an alien, nor borrow,
I yield it thee freely, come better or worse.
(from Anon. "The Famine in Ireland", qtd. in Burke & Woods 31–2)

A small but memorable insight into the impact of the Great Famine comes from the pen of a German travel writer, Moritz Hartmann (1821–72), who visited Ireland in 1850. "Ireland's poverty is quite beyond belief", he wrote; "what it means for people to be desolate and annihilated I only now know" (qtd. in Bourke, *"Poor Green Erin"* 518). He adapted lines from Shakespeare's *Romeo and Juliet* (Act V, Scene 1) in an attempt to convey the depth of his feeling at what he had witnessed (qtd. in Bourke, *"Poor Green Erin"* 518):

Famine is in thy cheeks,
Need and oppression starveth in thine eyes
Contempt and beggary hang upon thy back;
The world is not thy friend, nor the world's law.[10]

Another German writer, the poet Ferdinand Freiligrath (whose work was translated into English by James Clarence Mangan, who also translated some of Whitman's poems into German), wrote about the Famine in his 1847 poem "Ireland" (Freiligrath 213):

The boat swings to a rusty chain;

The sail, the oar of use no longer;
The fisher boy died yester-e'en,

And now the father faints with hunger.
Pale Ireland's fish is landlord's fish,
[....]
His gold makes gaming-tables glitter.
The while his Irish poor lie down
And die, like flies in bitter winter.

In another stanza of the same long poem that begins "The landlord cares for fox and hound", Freiligrath accuses the landlords of Ireland of leaving the land to "the rabbit / and the screaming plover – / Their worth a peasant's worth surpasses" (Freiligrath 214).[11]

Figure 8 | Hughie O'Donoghue, *On Our Knees*

AFTER THE DIGGING: A MODERN AMERICAN RESPONSE

One of the most original sequences of poetry to explore the complex moral and ethical implications of the Great Famine was written by Jewish American poet Alan Shapiro. His 1981 collection *After the Digging* is divided into two sections, the first focusing on the Famine in Ireland, the second on demonic possession in late seventeenth-century New England. As a whole these poems consider the nature of human complicity in helping to create the conditions for events like the Famine and the New England witch trials, moral realms and human actions parallel to those of the twentieth century that gave rise to Hannah Arendt's famous concept the "banality of evil".

Shapiro's Famine poems were inspired by his reading of *The Irish Question*, a column in the London *Times* that began in 1846 in response to the Famine. "What fascinated me", Shapiro writes, "was not so much the journalistic accounts of what was going on in Ireland, the suffering that the Irish endured between 1846 and 1849, but how the English perceived and responded to a devastation their own economic, social, and political policies had helped create and prolong" (Shapiro 35). At the same time as he was reading those newspaper columns (summer 1978), Shapiro read *The Great Hunger* by Cecil Woodham-Smith, and says that this "graphic description and analysis of the catastrophe", together with the newspaper accounts, "comprised much of the materials, voices and idioms" he would use in composing the Irish section of *After the Digging*.

In the afterword to a later edition of the collection, Shapiro writes:

My ambition in these poems was to explore how decent people can be brought to do indecent things ... By adopting the personae of certain nineteenth-century English officials who observed the horrible consequences of their policies and attitudes, and various seventeenth-century New England Puritans blinded by fanatical obsession, I tried to dramatize and embody the fragility and contingency of moral norms, and the insidious ways perception, action and intimate feelings are constrained, if not entirely determined, by the pressures of history (Shapiro 36).

Shapiro cites "the many evils of the 20th century" as the spur for writing about the Irish Famine and the New England witch trials: the two world wars, the Holocaust, and the atomic-bomb attacks on Hiroshima and Nagasaki. Noting that he has addressed some of these themes more directly in later work, he hopes "the voices of the more recent dead will now be available in the historically remote but still compelling voices brought together in *After the Digging*" (Shapiro 36).

> *Last week outside of Erris where*
> *the poor like crows swarm, combing the black fields,*
> *living on nettles, weeds, and cabbage leaves,*
> *women and children plundered a meal cart,*
> *fifteen of them tearing at the sacks;*
> *enlivened rags, numb to the drivers' whips,*
> *too weak to drag the sacks off, or to scream,*
> *they hobbled away, clutching to themselves*
> *only small handfuls of the precious stuff.*
>
> *Please do not think me impudent. Like you*
> *I feel no great affection for the Irish.*
> *But it is not enough that "we should tell them*
> *they suffer from the providence of God";*
> *or that "in terms of economic law*
> *it's beneficial that the price of grain*
> *should rise in proportion to the drop in wage."*
> *We can no longer answer cries of want*
> *with quoting economics, or with prayer.*
> *Ireland is not, and never can be, Whitehall.*
> *And while they starve, no Englishman is safe.*
>
> *Sir, you have said yourself, "The evil here*
> *with which we must contend is not the famine,*
> *but their turbulent and selfish character,"*
> *which I half think Nature herself condemns:*
> *today, as if from the Old Testament –*
> *with thunder beating on the iron clouds*
> *which do not bend – the electricity*
> *strikes with the bright and jagged edge of judgment,*
> *while over each blighted field a dense fog falls*
> *cold and damp and close, without any wind.*
> (from "Randolf Routh to Charles Trevelyan", Shapiro 3–4)

HEARTSLOPES OF CONNECTION

To draw parallels between the Great Famine of Ireland and the Holocaust is to risk accusations of simplification and exaggeration, but as Christopher Morash has pointed out, the bureaucratic nature of evil during the Third Reich has certain parallels with the administration of Poor Law relief in the Famine years (35). Poetry *was* possible after Auschwitz, and, indeed, one could argue that it was more essential than ever in the aftermath of the Holocaust. Poets such as Primo Levi, Nelly Sachs, and Paul Celan bore witness to the suffering of their people, and in some of their poems one can read of the suffering of all people who have been starved, persecuted, and driven to their deaths. Celan's "The Broached Year" articulates the hunger beyond hunger of all famished people: "The broached year / with its mouldering crusts / of delusion bread. / Drink / from my mouth" (Celan 104). Another of his poems, "Irish", connects Ireland to one of the enduring songs of protest and defiance from the concentration camps, "The Peat Bog Soldiers", or "Borgermoor Lied" ("We are the peat bog soldiers / Marching with our spades to the moor"). Paul Robeson sang "The Peat Bog Soldiers", and the Irish singer Mary McPartlan sings a memorable version of it, her voice evoking images of the Famine Irish toiling on so-called relief roads (some across bogland) to earn the right to eat. Celan's poem is a vision of post-trauma peace, the bogland of Ireland reclaimed as a place of consolation and healing.

Irish

Give me the right of way
over the corn steps into your sleep,
the right of way
over the sleep path
the right to cut peat
on the heart slope,
tomorrow.
(Celan 92)

THE SPACES BETWEEN: POETRY OF FAMINE PROSE

A striking aspect of the broader literary legacy from the Great Hunger is the extent to which novelists and playwrights have created memorable prose poetry in their exploration of the Famine and its legacy.

In her novel *Still Waters in Niger*, American writer Kathleen Hill (all of whose great-grandparents emigrated from Ireland to the US in the years following the Famine) meditates on the power of individual and communal memory within the context of contemporary famine in Niger in West Africa, and gently challenges given perceptions of place, time, and mother–daughter relationships while steering the power of the novel towards the realm of poetry. This work also draws a clear line of connection between Ireland's Great Hunger and the ongoing reality of famine and hunger-death in many African countries:

Sa zuciya ga ci, shi ya kawo jin yunwa.
It is setting the heart on eating that brings on hunger.

How to speak to the silences, the spaces between?

[...]
There is too much in a single day, a superfluity that dulls the senses. What are we to do with it all, the sun breaking on the roof and sand, the footsteps in the street, the silver flash of a bird's wing? ... / There is both too much and much, much too little. And what we have, the brimming world itself, does not always include the indispensable potato, rotting in the field (Hill 160–1).

Tom Murphy's 1977 play *Famine* reaches towards poetic language and expression to articulate the deep *caoin*, or cry of grief, for the death of a young woman in the village of Glanconor in "rural Ireland" in autumn 1846, the words and sounds crossing from one language to another, and in turn becoming a kind of lament for the loss of a language itself (Murphy 11).

Cold and silent is now her bed;
Damp is the blessed dew of night,
But the sun will bring warmth and heat in the morning
and dry up the dew
But her heart will feel no heat from the sun.
Nor no more the tracks of her feet in the dew.
Nor the sound of her step in the Village of Connor,
Where she was ever foremost among young women.
No!
Cold and silent is now her bed.
Yes.[12]

A book loved by Seamus Heaney, David Thomson's memoir *Woodbrook*, details local Famine memory from County Roscommon with the power and rhythm of poetry. The world of Woodbrook – its people and the remembered connection to the Great Hunger – is evoked in a poem by Joseph Woods published in the *Irish Times* (February 6, 2016), "Eternal Rest at Ardcarne Cemetery", which remembers the farm workers, landowners, and Famine victims interred there:

[...] Underneath, a democracy of dead:
Tommy Maxwell, the MacDermotts,
the King-Harmons and the two
to three interred daily for the first
seven weeks of black forty seven.

Figure 9 | Joseph Haverty, *The Blind Piper*

WRITING POEMS OF FAMINE

The landscape of north Leitrim and south Roscommon invoked in Thomson's writing inspired some of my own poems on themes of Famine memory, loss, and concealment. Impending hunger is a cloak for calculated killing in "Famine Pit" (Woods, *Lives and Miracles* 49–51), which tells the story of a man who kills his stepchildren by throwing them down a disused mineshaft, clearing the way for his son's inheritance. This hard story was retained in folk memory and passed directly to me by my mother and a neighbor, a coal miner from the area in which the events happened.

I offer a small glimmer of possible hope in "Famine Pit": "Some had it one of the girls got frightened / Before they reached the pit and ran off; She stayed with her father's people /And went to America when she was fifteen" (Woods, *Lives and Miracles* 50). This ambiguous offering of survival and renewal mirrors an image in another of my poems, "The Piper in the Snow" (McLean 222), inspired by Joseph Haverty's 1844 painting *The Blind Piper* **[Figure 9]** in the National Gallery of Ireland:

The Piper in the Snow

The piper played a reel:
"Na Prátaí Geala Bána"
The young girl danced
And there was no tomorrow

He knew her by her step;
Sometimes he'd say,
Your feet, a stór, will dance
Across the sea

That blighted winter
Lying in the snow
He knew he felt her hands
Upon his hair

And heard her voice
Unaltered –
O think will there be music
Over there?

In inventing a tune title – "Na Prátaí Geala Bána" ("The Shining White Potatoes") – I wanted to raise an echo of the song "Na Prátaí Dubha", imagining a tune in celebration and praise of the food that gave such sustenance and comfort before the calamity of blight.

The image of a gift of music and song carried to the New World on the tide of post-Famine migration is present in the work of Connemara poet Mary O'Malley, who has explored themes of famine and forged links to a wider world of linguistic and cultural loss and contemporary poverty and inequality in poems like "The Abandoned Child", "In the Name of God and of the Dead Generations" ("We have spent a small ransom / remembering the famine / that some of us never forgot / in Universities all over America" (O'Malley, *Asylum Road* 25)), and "The Boning Hall". In her poem "Famine Grass" (O'Malley, *Knife in the Wave* 49), she imagines the voice of the great Connemara *sean-nós* singer Seosamh Ó hEanaigh (Joe Heaney) carrying a freight of history and healing from the west of Ireland to the new world of New York City:

He soaked it all in –
The generations of dead and banished
Had left words after them, chain-linked
From Rosmuc to Barna.
They waited to be voiced
Shivering in the folds of hills,
Leaning against gables,
Like old men, or drowned
At the mouth of every bay
From Bertraboy to Carna:
Famine grass, American wake, coffin ship.
He said them among half-sets and jigs
And set Cearbhaill's love song
Wandering down the centuries.

A SHADOW ON THE HEART: CONTEMPORARY WRITERS

The link between poetry and music in exploring the history and impact of the Great Hunger comes to the fore in the work of songwriter Shane MacGowan, whose admiration for the work of James Clarence Mangan has fueled his unique exploration of the Famine-haunted landscapes of Ireland in a song like "Down in the Ground Where the Dead Men Go". These lyrics may be considered in the context of a merging of poetic and ballad traditions, and the creation of a nightmarish *aisling*, or vision poem: "Walking home three parts pissed / I fell and rolled in the morning mist / I fell and tumbled in the hungry grass / That tells the tale of a terrible past / I screamed and rolled and dreamt I fell / Down in the depths of a freezing hell".[13] (For a complete picture of song as witness and remembrance in relation to *An Gorta Mór*, see Mick Moloney's *Across the Western Ocean: Songs of Leaving and Arriving* in this Famine Folio series.)

Poets in Ireland, the US, and Australia continue to explore terrains of memory and loss in relation to the Famine. In Australia, Sydney poet Colleen Burke has written several poems that reference aspects of the Famine, one of the most striking being "A Shadow on the Heart", where the poet holds a potato in her hand and knows the "near death of a people / their spirit" (Burke 166). In her collection *Marrowbone of Memory: Ireland's Great Famine*, Appalachian poet Jeri McCormick draws on generational stories of the Famine, imagining the voices and witnessed experiences of a myriad of people from orphan girl to undertaker, and uses an epigraph from New York writer Peter Quinn in the title poem (13):

> *Recalled or unrecalled, memory is embedded*
> *in the way we love, hope, believe ...*
> *it will not disappear.*

The building of a substantial *oeuvre* of poetry relating to the Great Hunger continues in Ireland. Desmond Egan attempts to link modern malaise and political corruption to the country's Famine past in his collection *Famine* (with drawings by James McKenna), originally published in 1997. The old potato ridges, or lazy beds, of the west and western islands of Ireland are painted into clear light by Eva Bourke in her poem "Trip to an Island": "Imagine fields as text / and you could read these furrows [...] / word by word and sentence by sentence / as an island people's epic. / Every noun or verb unearthed,/turned over and over again/in the harsh light of hunger" (Bourke, *Spring in Henry Street* 78–9). Micheal O'Siadhail considers the links between Ireland's Famine history and a wide world of contemporary hunger and suffering in work like "Crying Out": "A history of our world unravels into histories, / The crying out of once forgotten stories, / The mended reed of voices we've refound / Proclaiming all that was trampled underground. / But out of our darkest silences now instead / We risk becoming everything we dread" (O'Siadhail 620).

Figure 10 | Jay Murphy, *All That Remains*

A SKEIN OF CONNECTION

The art collection at the Great Hunger Museum at Quinnipiac University has already inspired a poem by Zen Buddhist priest Myozan Kodo (Ian Kilroy), while John F. Deane's poem "Slievemore: The Abandoned Village" is displayed alongside Geraldine O'Reilly's *Deserted Village, Achill Island*. Ezra Pound's dictum "Make it New" informed my decision to ask Eiléan Ní Chuilleanáin to write a poem for this publication **[Figure 12]**; her words honor a little-known detail from late in the life of the Irish novelist Maria Edgeworth **[Figure 11]**, who knitted balaclavas for the New York stevedores loading ships to carry food relief to Famine-stricken Ireland **[Figure 13]**.

Maria Edgeworth in 1847

She was touched by the generosity of the porters who carried the rice and India meal to the vessels for shipment to Ireland in the famine, refusing all payment; and she knit with her own hands a woollen comforter for each porter, of bright and pretty colours, which she sent to a friend to present to the men, who were proud and grateful for the gifts; but, alas! before they received them, those kind hands were cold, and that warm heart had ceased to beat (*A Memoir of Maria Edgeworth* by Frances Edgeworth).

Anger. Work. Confusion – what is to be done?
– the Atlantic in the way and the news getting worse,
work stretching to occupy every hour in the day,
carrying back and forth, lifting bearing and setting down.

We are in the centuries when work told the body
how to lift, fasten and drag, the weight of the world needed heaving,
when the horses staggered and slowed on the steep hill
the coach too full, too heavy to drag onwards –

they stopped fearfully and the child from the cabin
was waiting for his chance, he ran out with a stone,
pushed it behind the wheel so the horses could breathe
and waited for the farthings flung from the passengers' windows.

Now he is carrying sacks of meal to the boat,
back and forth, loaded then free, and the work stretching ahead
like the road where at the same moment Maria Edgeworth
walks out, her young servant beside her carrying

the basket that gets a bit lighter
at every cabin door. This is her work now
at the end of her life. At home,
she sits down to the story she is writing

line after line, her hand straying back and forth
across her remaining pages. The child from the cabin
is a man carrying meal to the docks, and at last
the day is over, and time for him to be paid –

but he is too angry, his comrades are too angry
to take money for helping to feed starving people. And she
who is not ever recorded as being angry
takes out her knitting needles and the long skeins of wool

the women have spun in the cabins, to make
a warm comforter for every man, her needles
twitching back and forth until the work is done.
She is famous and fortunate, she will be remembered.

Like the girl whose brothers were turned into swans,
she does what she knows, the long scarves piling
softly beside her chair, one after the other like the days.

They are far from home when her gift reaches them, the trace
of their work unravelling like a worn thread of wool, their kindness
out of anger stretching across the sea, and answered.

Figure 11 | Richard Beard, *Maria Edgeworth*

Maria Edgeworth in 1847

Anger. Work. Confusion – what is to be done?
– the Atlantic in the way and the news getting worse,
work stretching to occupy every hour in the day,
carrying back and forth, lifting bearing and setting down.

We are in the centuries when work told the body
how to lift, fasten and drag, the weight of the world needed heaving,
when the horses staggered and slowed on the steep hill,
the coach too full, too heavy to drag onwards –

they stopped fearfully and the child from the cabin
was waiting for his chance, he ran out with a stone,
pushed it behind the wheel so the horses could breathe
and waited for the farthings flung from the passengers' windows.

Now he is carrying sacks of meal to the boat,
back and forth, loaded then free, and the work stretching ahead
like the road where at the same moment Maria Edgeworth
walks out, her young servant beside her carrying

the basket that gets a bit lighter
at every cabin door. This is her work now
at the end of her life. At home,
she sits down to the story she is writing

line after line, her hand straying back and forth
across her remaining pages. The child from the cabin
is a man carrying meal to the docks, and at last
the day is over, and time for him to be paid –

Figure 12 | "Maria Edgeworth in 1847" by Eiléan Ní Chuilleanáin

but he is too angry, his comrades are too angry
to take money for helping to feed starving people. And she
who is not ever recorded as being angry
takes out her knitting needles and the long skeins of wool

the women have spun in the cabins, to make
a warm comforter for every man, her needles
twitching back and forth until the work is done.
She is famous and fortunate, she will be remembered.

Like the girl whose brothers were turned into swans,
she does what she knows, the long scarves piling
softly beside her chair, one after the other like the days.

They are far from home when her gift reaches them, the trace
of their work unravelling like a worn thread of wool, their kindness
out of anger stretching across the sea, and answered.

Eiléan Ní Chuilleanáin

'She was touched by the generosity of the porters who carried the rice and Indian meal to the vessels for shipment to Ireland in the famine, refusing all payment, and she knit with her own hands a woollen comforter for each porter, of bright and pretty colours, which she sent to a friend to present to the men, who were proud and grateful for the gifts; but alas! before they received them, those kind hands were cold, and that warm heart had ceased to beat.'

A memoir of Maria Edgeworth by Frances Edgeworth

Figure 13 | "Loading and Unloading, Pier No. 6, East River" (*Harper's Weekly*, September 1877)

STALKS TO THE LIGHT

"Poems are the memory of the world", an old Vietnamese man tells the Danish writer Karsten Jensen in his book *I Have Seen the World Begin*. The poems of the Great Hunger remember the past, but they are also a vital act of grace that helps makes the present bearable and the future possible.

The leaves of hungry grass are green, tough, enduring. The words are stalks to the light. The dead are not forgotten.

ENDNOTES

[1] Christopher Morash, email to Vincent Woods, May 2016.

[2] Christoper Morash gives a fascinating account of Yeats's complex exploration of Famine themes and legacies in his 2014 article "Where all ladders start': Famine memories in Yeats's *Countess Cathleen*", in Corporaal et al., *Global Legacies of the Great Irish Famine*.

[3] Michael Coady, email to Vincent Woods, January 2016.

[4] Ibid.

[5] In "The Divided Mind" (40), Thomas Kinsella writes: "When Patrick Kavanagh introduced a broadcast of The Great Hunger some years ago, and confessed with his usual forthrightness that the work 'is not completely born ... You must have technique, architecture', his self-knowledge was punishing, and his self-judgement heroic."

[6] Fintan O'Toole, "Modern Ireland in 100 artworks: 1942: 'The Great Hunger', by Patrick Kavanagh", *Irish Times*, May 16, 2015.

[7] *Poets' Offering* program, August 25, 1968 (Dublin: Dolmen Press, 1968). The copy reproduced in this publication is from the Pearse Hutchinson Archive at Maynooth University, Ireland.

[8] Adrienne Leavy, "Thomas Kinsella: eliciting order from significant experience", *Irish Times*, January 13, 2016, originally published in *Reading Ireland: The Little Magazine* 1.3 (fall 2015), www.readingireland.net (accessed May 11, 2016).

[9] In addition to her own work and research published in *Muse as Maid*, Aífe Murray also cites references in two other books for Margaret Maher's role in saving Dickinson's poems: Martha Dickinson Bianchi, *Emily Dickinson Face to Face* (Boston, MA: Houghton Mifflin, 1932), and Polly Longsworth, *Austin and Mabel: The Amherst Affair and Love Letters of Austin Dickinson and Mabel Loomis Todd* (New York: Farrar, Straus, and Giroux, 1984) detail Maher's part in protecting Dickinson's poems, which had been stored in the Irish woman's trunk.

[10] The Moritz Hartmann text is just one of many fascinating insights into life and conditions in Ireland in the early nineteenth century in Eoin Bourke's book *"Poor Green Erin": German Travel Writers' Narratives on Ireland from Before the 1798 Rising to After the Great Famine* (Frankfurt: Peter Lang, 2011). All the texts were edited, translated, and annotated by Eoin Bourke, who quotes Hartmann's friend Fanny Lewald describing "a bitter yell of despair about Irish conditions" in a letter Hartmann wrote to her from Dublin in 1850 (Bourke *"Poor Green Erin"* 518).

[11] Eoin Bourke made me aware of these poems, which were translated into English by Mary Howitt. The full texts are available in a selection of English translations of his work, *Poems: From the German of Ferdinand Freiligrath*, ed. Kate Freiligrath-Kroeke, 2nd edn (Leipzig: Bernard Tauchnitz, 1871).

[12] In Tom Murphy's play *Famine*, the words I reproduce as poetry (because they constitute a pure run of poetry) can be found in Scene 1, "The Wake", and are spoken by Dan O'Dea's wife, John Connor's wife (Mother), and a chorus of neighbors, who are attending the wake of John Connor's daughter in the village of Glanconor on a Sunday afternoon in the autumn of 1846.

[13] The full text of "Down in the Ground Where the Dead Men Go" is published in *Poguetry: The Lyrics of Shane MacGowan* (London: Faber & Faber, 1989).

WORKS CITED

Berkeley Tolchin, Sarah. "Famine Cottages". *What Just Happened*. Oldcastle, County Meath: Gallery Press, 2015. Republished in *Windharp: Poems of Ireland Since 1916*. Ed. Niall MacMonagle. 292.

Boland, Eavan. *Code*. Manchester: Carcanet Press, 2001.

---. *New Collected Poems*. Manchester: Carcanet Press, 2005.

Bourke, Eoin. *"Poor Green Erin": German Travel Writers' Narratives on Ireland from Before the 1798 Rising to After the Great Famine*. Frankfurt: Peter Lang, 2011.

Bourke, Eva. "Trip to an Island". *Spring in Henry Street*. Dublin: Dedalus Press, 1996.

Burke, Colleen. *Home Brewed and Lethal: New and Selected Poems, 1974-1997*. Maleny, Queensland: Cochon Publishing, 1997.

Burke, Colleen Z. and Vincent Woods. *The Turning Wave: Poems and Songs of Irish Australia*. Armidale, NSW: Kardoorair Press, 2001.

Celan, Paul. "The Broached Year" and "Irish". *Selected Poems*. Trans. Michael Hamburger and Christoper Middleton. Harmondsworth, Middlesex: Penguin Books, 1972.

Coady, Michael. "Na Prátaí Dubha/The Blackened Potatoes". *All Souls*. Oldcastle, County Meath: Gallery Press, 1997.

Corporaal, Marguérite, Christopher Cusack, Lindsay Janssen, and Ruud van den Beuken. Eds. *Global Legacies of the Great Irish Famine: Transnational and Interdisciplinary Perspectives*. Reimagining Ireland 60. Oxford: Peter Lang, 2014.

Deane John. "Slievemore: The Abandoned Village". *A Little Book of Hours*. Manchester: Carcanet Press, 2008.

Durcan, Paul. "What Shall I Wear, Darling, to *The Great Hunger*?". *A Snail in My Prime: Selected Poems*. London: Harvill Press, 1993.

Egan, Desmond. "Famine VII". *Famine*. Newbridge, County Kildare: Goldsmith Press, 1997 & 2012.

Freiligrath, Ferdinand. *Poems: From the German of Ferdinand Freiligrath*. Ed. Kate Freiligrath-Kroeke. 2nd edn. Leipzig: Bernard Tauchnitz, 1871.

French, Tom. "A Cauldron in Dunshaughlin". *Midnightstown*. Oldcastle, County Meath: Gallery Press, 2014.

Heaney, Seamus. "At a Potato Digging". *Death of a Naturalist*. London: Faber & Faber, 1966 & 2006.

Hewitt, John. "The Scar". *The Collected Poems of John Hewitt*. Ed. Frank Ormsby. Belfast: Blackstaff Press, 1991.

Hill, Kathleen. *Still Waters in Niger*. Evanston, IL: TriQuarterly Books/Northwestern University Press, 1999.

Hutchinson, Pearse. "Pibroch". *Collected Poems*. Oldcastle, County Meath: Gallery Press, 2002.

---. "Gorta". Pearse Hutchinson Archive, Maynooth University. Trans. Vincent Woods.

Jensen, Carsten. *I Have Seen the World Begin*. London: Harvill Press, 2002.

Kavanagh, Patrick. "The Great Hunger". *Collected Poems*. Ed. Antoinette Quinn. London: Penguin Classics, 2005.

Kinsella, Thomas. "The Divided Mind". *Prose Occasions, 1951–2006*. Ed. Andrew Fitzsimons. Manchester: Carcanet Press, 2009.

Kinsella, Thomas. "From the Land of the Dead". *Collected Poems, 1956-2001*. Manchester: Carcanet Press, 2001.

Kodo, Myozan (Ian Kilroy). *Three Rock Sonnets*. Zen Buddhism Ireland, 2013.

Krieg, Joann P. *Walt Whitman and the Irish*. Iowa City, IA: University of Iowa Press, 2000.

Leavy, Adrienne. "Thomas Kinsella: eliciting order from significant experience". *Irish Times*. January 13, 2016. Originally published in *Reading Ireland: The Little Magazine*.

McCormick, Jeri. *Marrowbone of Memory: Ireland's Great Famine*. Cliffs of Moher, County Clare: Salmon Poetry, 2013.

MacDonagh, Donagh, "The Hungry Grass". *The Hungry Grass*. London: Faber & Faber, 1947.

McLean, Janet. *Lines of Vision: Irish Writers on Art*. Ed. Janet McLean. London: Thames & Hudson, 2014.

McMonagle, Niall. Ed. *Windharp: Poems of Ireland Since 1916.* Dublin: Penguin Ireland, 2016.

Morash Christopher. *The Hungry Voice: The Poetry of the Irish Famine.* Dublin: Irish Academic Press, 1989.

Murphy Thomas. *Famine*. Dublin: Gallery Press, 1977.

Murray Aífe. *Maid as Muse: How Servants Changed Emily Dickinson's Life and Language*. Lebanon, NH: University of New Hampshire Press, 2009.

Murray, Martin G. *Pete the Great: A Biography of Peter Doyle*. Walt Whitman Archive. http://whitmanarchive.org/criticism/current/anc.00155.html (accessed January 1, 2016). Originally published in *Walt Whitman Quarterly Review* 12 (summer 1994).

O'Connor, Nuala. *Miss Emily*. Ross-shire, Scotland: Sandstone Press, 2015.

Ó Gráda, Cormac and Diarmaid Ó Muirithe: "The famine of 1740–41: representations in Gaelic poetry". *Éire-Ireland* 45.3–4 (fall/winter 2010).

O'Malley, Mary. "Famine Grass". *The Knife in the Wave*. Cliffs of Moher, County Clare: Salmon Poetry, 1997.

---. "In the Name of God and of the Dead Generations". *Asylum Road*. Cliffs of Moher, County Clare: Salmon Poetry, 2001.

---. "The Boning Hall". *The Boning Hall: New and Selected Poems*. Manchester: Carcanet Press, 2002.

O'Siadhail, Micheal. "Crying Out". *Collected Poems*. Tarset, Northumberland: Bloodaxe Books, 2013.

Poets' Offering program, August 25, 1968. Dublin: Dolmen Press, 1968.

Ryan, Richard. "Famine Village". Originally published in *Ledges*. Dublin: Dolmen Press, 1970. Republished in McMonagle (ed.), *Windharp* 80.

Shapiro, Alan. "Randolph Routh to Charles Trevelyan" and quotations from afterword. *After the Digging*. Chicago, IL: University of Chicago Press, 1998.

Szymborska Wislawa "The End and the Beginning". *View with a Grain of Sand: Selected Poems*. London: Faber & Faber, 1996.

Thomson, David. *Woodbrook*. London: Vintage, 1994.

Whitman, Walt. "Old Ireland". *Selected Poems: 1855–1892*. Ed. Gary Schmidgall. New York: St. Martin's Griffin, 1999.

Woods, Joseph. "Eternal Rest, Ardcarne Cemetery". *Irish Times*. February 6, 2016.

Woods, Vincent. "Famine Pit". *Lives and Miracles*. Galway: Arlen House, 2002.

---. "The Piper in the Snow", *Lines of Vision: Irish Writers on Art*. Ed. Janet McLean. London: Thames & Hudson, 2014.

Yeats, William Butler. *The Dreaming of the Bones* and *The Countess Cathleen. Collected Plays*. London: Macmillan, 1982.

---. "The Circus Animals' Desertion". *W.B. Yeats: Poems Selected by Seamus Heaney*. London: Faber & Faber, 2004.

IMAGES

Cover
Brian Maguire
b. 1951
The World is Full of Murder
1985
Acrylic on canvas
53 x 86 in (134.6 x 218.4 cm)
© Brian Maguire, 1985
Image provided by Ireland's Great Hunger Museum, Quinnipiac University

Figure 1
Miriam de Búrca
b. 1972
Famine Sod from Tarmon, Co. Leitrim
2015
Ink on man-made vellum
19.7 x 27.6 in (50 x 70 cm)
© Miriam de Búrca

Figure 2
Women Breaking Stones on Achill Island
c. 1800s
Formerly in collection of Alexander Williams RHA (1846–1930)
Image provided by John O'Shea

Figure 3
Famine-relief road: the road to nowhere, Bluestack Mountains, Lough Eske, County Donegal
Photograph by Patsy McNulty

Figure 4
Daniel Macdonald
1820–53
An Irish Peasant Family Discovering the Blight of their Store
1847
Oil on canvas
33 x 41 in (84 x 104 cm)
Image provided by National Folklore Collection, University College, Dublin

Figure 5
Patrick Kavanagh picking potatoes, Inniskeen, Co. Monaghan
1963
8.7 x 6.5 in (22 x 16.5 cm)
Wiltshire Photographic Collection
National Library of Ireland

Figure 6
Program for *Poets' Offering*
Abbey Theatre, Dublin
August 25, 1968

Figure 7
Lilian Lucy Davidson
1879–1954
Gorta
1946
Previously known as ***Burying the Child***
Oil on canvas
27.5 x 35.5 in (69.9 x 90.2 cm)
© Estate of Lilian Lucy Davidson
Image provided by Ireland's Great Hunger Museum, Quinnipiac University

Figure 8
Hughie O'Donoghue
b. 1953
On Our Knees
1995
Watercolor
40 x 60 in (101.6 x 152.4 cm)
© Hughie O'Donoghue, 1995
Image provided by Ireland's Great Hunger Museum, Quinnipiac University

Figure 9
Joseph Haverty
1794–1864
The Blind Piper
1841
Oil on canvas
29.9 x 23.2 in (76 x 59 cm)
Photo © National Gallery of Ireland

Figure 10
Jay Murphy
b. 1952
All That Remains
1995
Mixed media
22.5 x 19 in (57.2 x 48.3 cm)
© Jay Murphy, 2012
Image provided by Ireland's Great Hunger Museum, Quinnipiac University

Figure 11
Richard Beard
1801–85
Maria Edgeworth (1768–1849)
1841
Daguerreotype
2.125 x 1.75 in (5.4 x 4.4 cm)
© National Portrait Gallery, London

Figure 12
"Maria Edgeworth in 1847"
By Eiléan Ní Chuilleanáin
2016

Figure 13
"Loading and Unloading, Pier No. 6, East River"
Harper's Weekly
September, 1877
Picture Collection, The New York Public Library, Astor, Lenox and Tilden Foundations

ACKNOWLEDGMENTS

My grateful thanks to Deirdre Cronin for her invaluable help in the development of this essay; to Kevin Barry and Maurice Walsh for their close reading and advice; and to Miriam de Burca, Michael Coady, and Eiléan Ní Chuilleanáin for their special contributions to the folio.

ABOUT THE AUTHOR

Vincent Woods is a poet, playwright, and broadcaster. His plays include *At the Black Pig's Dyke* (1992) and *A Cry from Heaven* (2005); his radio plays include *The Gospels of Aughamore* (2004) and *Broken Moon* (2012); his poetry collections are *The Colour of Language* (1996) and *Lives and Miracles* (2002). He co-edited, with Colleen Burke, *The Turning Wave: Poems and Songs of Irish Australia* (2001). Some of his poems on the theme of famine and migration feature in *The Leitrim Equation 4* concert performance and DVD (2016). He has received the Stewart Parker award for drama, and the Ted McNulty award for poetry. He has presented many arts programs on RTÉ Radio (Irish national broadcaster), and has been writer-in-residence at National University of Ireland, Galway. He is a member of Aosdána, the Irish academy of artists.

SERIES EDITORS

Niamh O'Sullivan
Grace Brady

IMAGE RESEARCH

Claire Puzarne

DESIGN

Rachel Foley

ACKNOWLEDGMENT

Office of Public Affairs, Quinnipiac University

PUBLISHER

Quinnipiac University Press

PRINTING

GRAPHYCEMS

ISBN 978-0-9978374-4-5

Ireland's Great Hunger Museum
Quinnipiac University

3011 Whitney Avenue
Hamden, CT 06518-1908
203-582-6500

www.ighm.org